The Sevenfold Path To Peace

The Sevenfold Path To Peace

SEVEN LENTEN SERMONS

ALAN BACON BOND

THE SEVENFOLD PATH TO PEACE

Copyright © 1986 by
The C.S.S. Publishing Company, Inc.
Lima, Ohio

All rights reserved. No part of this publication may be reproduced, stored in a retrieval system, or transmitted in any form or by any means, electronic, mechanical, photocopying, recording, or otherwise, without the prior permission of the publisher. Inquiries should be addressed to: The C.S.S. Publishing Company, Inc., 628 South Main Street, Lima, Ohio 45804.

6801 / ISBN 0-89536-774-2

Table of Contents

Preface 7

First Week in Lent
"Is Peace Attainable?" 11

Second Week in Lent
"Desire Peace" 15

Third Week in Lent
"Peacemaking — Active, Not Passive" ... 21

Fourth Week in Lent
"Peace as Shalom" 27

Fifth Week in Lent
"The Gift of Peace" 35

Sixth Week in Lent (Palm Sunday)
"Peace Through Sacrifice" 43

Easter Sunday
"Proclaim Peace" 49

Preface

The 1981 General Synod of the United Church of Christ chose *Peace* as one of the denomination's priorities for the next biennium. The means of engaging our local congregation in the worship of God while creating sermons is to suggest the topic, together with Biblical material, at a mid-week potluck breakfast. The participants engage in reflections on the theme, while the pastor takes notes on the discussion. The remarks, more often than not, provide illustrative material and direction for the sermon preparation, but the real worth is found in the fact that the participants in that mid-week event come to the Sunday worship with a sense of anticipation and orientation to the theme of the service.

In the course of the worship itself, the congregation is afforded an opportunity to address the topic during so-called "Moments of Reflection."

The people are invited to listen to a passage of Scripture, "keeping in mind the topic of the Moments of Reflection." Following the reading, they are encouraged with the following words: "In light of the reading we have heard, and as inspired by the Holy Spirit, what comes to your mind when you think of the (topic)?" Members of the congregation then respond with brief phrases which the pastor repeats for all to hear. This portion of the worship occurs in a period prior to the sermon. It gives the congregation the first word and orients them to the topic. During the sermon the speaker may then affirm some of those remarks.

The organization and title of these sermons grew out of the fact that they were prepared for the Lenten to Easter season, which has seven Sundays. Your reading of this series will be greatly enhanced by reading the Scripture passages and reflecting on the hymns, listed prior to each sermon, and by making personal notes on the subject of the Moments of Reflection.

The deep gratitude of the author is expressed to the devout people who met for breakfast at 6:00 a.m. each Wednesday through Lent, sharing in the spiritual "benefits" of rising early and casting the day in the robes of faith. Especially instrumental in the process were Lois and Meg Bond, wife and daughter, who attended the breakfasts, meaning I did not need to dress in the dark; and Marion Inward, my secretary, whose good humor, attentive ear, and provocative questions provided a most helpful atmosphere in which to write, while sheltering me from interruption.

Unless otherwise noted, all Bible references are from the Revised Standard Version of the Bible. (Division of Christian Education of the National Council of Churches in the United States of America. Copyright 1946 and 1952.)

I pray that this offering will stimulate all of us to walk the "Sevenfold Path to Peace."

                                            Alan Bacon Bond
                                            Scottsdale, Arizona

Scripture:
Psalm 4
Mark 4:35-41
Judges 6:11-24
Philippians 4:1-10

Lent 1

"Is Peace Attainable?"

Text: *The Lord said to him, "Peace be to you; do not fear, you shall not die." Judges 6:23*

There was a storm on the sea during the night. Although that body of water would more rightly be called a lake, it has the capacity to produce violent waves. With the change in a weather front, the super-heated air over the desert sands to the east, start to rise, sucking up the cooler air from the Mediterranean like a vacuum cleaner across the hilly terrain of Galilee, with great turbulence striking the small inland sea, and then rushing up the looming Golan Heights.

Their thoughts and fear must have been like those of the eighty-five men on an oil rig in the North Sea, and the crew of a Soviet cargo vessel as they were struck and sunk by a gigantic winter storm. Total fear overwhelms. There is only one end in sight. Crashing waves. Gasping breath. A struggle upwards, unavailing; pleas to God. Yielding to the uncontrollable rage of elements — darkness . . . light . . . peace.

Perhaps there is something perverse in us which paradoxically yearns for the violence of the storm, in order that we might, at last, be brought to the inevitable peace of the stormy deep where, one day, we will join those who have passed through the storms of life. "Let's be on with it, be done with it, so, at last, we might rest in peace."

We hardly need rehearse the violence, wars, threats, and raging storms of our own time, to know there is no peace — no real enduring peace. Indeed, in the lifetime of a few of you, and through this century, when wars have been fought "to end all war," we have seemingly become more despairing of the prospect of achieving peace, or experiencing it, except by isolating ourselves from reality and from our responsibility for all of humanity.

There is a storm on the sea. We, like disciples in a Galilean boat, see our Teacher, Jesus, asleep on a cushion in the stern.

" 'Teacher, do you not care if we perish?' He awoke and rebuked the wind, and said to the sea, 'Peace. Be still!' and the wind ceased, and there was a great calm."

How shall we, who are living in the stormy seas of the 20th century, ever find such calm, experience such calm?

Eternal Father, Strong to save, whose arm doth bind the restless wave,
Who bidst the might ocean deep, its own appointed limits keep.
O hear us when we cry to thee for those in peril on the sea.

On this first week in Lent, as we have set out on a journey toward Easter, we are also beginning to explore the "Sevenfold Path to Peace." The urgency is obvious.

As we explore the "Sevenfold Path to Peace," it is not my intention, at the outset, to define what peace may or may not be, but instead to explore with you, during these Lenten days, the wilderness which exists between us and peace, in order that we might finally find it and eternally live it.

"Is peace attainable?"

If I despair — if I seem hopeless in regard to worldly probability — it is probably because there is in me, as I suspect in most of us, an unending feud. Perhaps it is best illustrated in the modern classic play and film *The Lion In Winter*.[1] Katherine Hepburn won an academy award for her performance of Eleanor of Acquitain in the film version. Set in 12th Century England, King Henry II has allowed his banished wife, Eleanor, a Christmas visit to see her sons, who are jealously anticipating which of them will ascend to Henry's throne.

In one scene, when the fraternal rivalry is reaching a fever pitch:

> Richard, going for his knife, says, "Why on earth wouldn't I?"
> John, the youngest brother (who has always felt that "father loves you more than me . . .") says, "A knife — he's got a knife."
> Eleanor: [How I wish I could imitate Hepburn's voice here!] Of course he has a knife. He always has a knife. We all have knives. it is eleven eighty-three, and we're barbarians. How clear we make it. Oh, my piglets, we're the origin of war. Not history's forces nor the times, nor justice, nor the lack of it. Nor causes, nor religions, nor ideas, nor kinds of government, nor any other thing.
> We are the killer; we breed war. We carry it, like syphilis, inside. Dead bodies rot in field and stream because the living ones are rotten. For the love of God, can't we love one another just a little?
> "That's how peace begins. We have so much to love each other for. We have such possibilities, my children, we could change the world."[2]

"We are the origins of war . . . for the love of God, can't we love one another just a little? That's how peace begins. We have so much to love each other for."

How well I know the origin of war. Recently I saw a sixth grader, on his way up the alley to school, throw a firecracker over the fence of our yard and into the chicken coop. I was as angry as I ever have been in my whole life. The chase was on! Down the alley, a hesitating wonder as to how he had vanished into thin air, spotting him darting from under a bush like a rabbit, over a five and a half foot wall, then over a six and a half foot back wall, I took the gate, across the church parking lot, and finally trapped him under the camper parked in a neighbor's yard. Winded and outraged, I yelled that I wanted to "kill" him, but instead took him to the school principal to do the disciplining. I didn't like the feeling that raged in me. I was even frightened by it. I certainly experienced the truth of the words of Eleanor of Aquitaine, "We are the origin of war."

I found some comfort when I returned to Psalm 4, previously chosen for this service,

> *Be angry but sin not . . . (and) in peace I will both lie down and sleep; for thou alone, O Lord, makest me dwell in safety.*

(Egg production dropped for a day, but neither the chickens nor the culprit died from the encounter!)

In a sermon on prayer, preached during the mid-1960's, Dr. Samuel Miller, Dean of Harvard Divinity School, described an idea that has been articulated in a number of places regarding the effect of what happens inside of us on the whole universe. Listen to him from the tape recording of that sermon. (Available from Word Inc.)

> *Prayer become possible in any world where everything, literally everything, from the farthest corner to the inmost center is completely and intricately woven together so that you cannot touch any one portion of the universe without there occurring a long series of infinite shocks and reverberations, like rings in a pool when a stone is thrown into it, and however minute and subtle these waves are, the entire universe is affected.*
>
> *"This is not particularly a resource of religious thinkers . . . a man like Alfred North Whitehead, has elevated this to what he calls the doctrine of the prehension of all things. Everything being bound in with every other thing, so that when you and I live by denials, or by anger, or by love, by any activity whatsoever, we're changing the universe, and changing at far greater distances than we have any idea.*

> *I presume that this is the kind of anger and hostility and bitterness and cynicism and hatred which you and I pile up in our souls and put down underneath the hatches, so our neighbors will not see it, and sometimes let loose against our loved one, who will forgive us. This kind of anger and hostility and bitterness and vengeance that we keep under the hatches until it accumulates so much that personally we dare not exhibit it, but some far off event in some other land may explode and all this hidden hostility rises and it is expressed patriotically in the defense of our own land against the enemy. It is the far-off wars that feed on your and my inner hostility, and anger and sin.*
>
> *It is true, it seems to me, that here at the very center of our world, there is this feeling of inter-wovenness and inter-relatedness so that we cannot do anything but that we put our finger on and move the world in one direction or another. And this is prayer. You are in communion with the universe. And no matter what you try to do to get out of communion, even your most stubborn denial and your most deliberate hostility and your most violent reaction still holds you with iron bands so that even in these things we change the world, not for the good, to be sure. But your prayers of evil are answered just as completely as your prayers of goodness.*[3]

No wonder there seems to be an escalating level of turmoil in our world! As we feed on war and mayhem in our consumption of news broadcasts and newspapers, we are generating winds of violence, throwing up stormy waves over the sea of humanity.

Jesus has something else in mind.

" 'Peace. Be still.' And the wind ceased and there was a great calm."

What do you have in mind?

Is peace attainable . . . in you . . . in us?

Your answer and mine will determine whether or not we are able to take the second step on the "Sevenfold Path to Peace."

Prayer

Eternal Father, strong to save, whose arm doth bind the mighty wave, there are storms which rage within us.

The winds of war toss up towering waves of fear. And we send out ever greater tidal waves which engulf the shores of other lands, and spread to the very limits of the universe.

"Peace. Be still," says the Lord. And the storm of jealousy, rivalry, hatred, sin, is still. There is a great calm. The sails lose the air and lie listless on the lake.

In the night one can hear the distant call of a bird, catch a scent of the earth, hear the splash of a jumping fish, and contemplate the depths of both sea and heaven.

Replace the fear in us, O God. Restore to our souls a new spirit of calm.

Establish us in truth . . . honor . . . justice . . . purity . . . loveliness . . . graciousness . . . the pursuit of excellence . . . the incentive to do those things which are worthy of praise.

Then let each of these ripple out from us, washing gently on the shore of other's lives, carrying in the gentle current of thought a similar attitude of peace, that, again and again, peace will ripple out, becoming a forceful current which transforms humanity, the world, the universe, in the name of Jesus. Amen

---

1. James Goldman, *The Lion in Winter*, (New York, Random House, 1965, used by permission).

2. *Ibid.* Act 1, Scene 5, p. 56.

3. From Catalyst Tape Talk, "Prayer" by Samuel Miller (Vol. 12, Number 10, ©1980, used by permission of Word Books, Publisher, Waco, TX 76796)

Scripture:
  Psalm 29
  Amos 5:18-24
  2 Peter 3:8-14

Lent 2

Desire Peace

Text: *Be zealous to be found by him without spot or blemish, and at peace.* **2 Peter 3:14**

If you were an astro-physicist from Kitt Peak Observatory, or a nuclear scientist from the Los Alamos Laboratory in New Mexico, how do you suppose you would interpret these words?

With a roar the sky will vanish, the elements will catch fire and fall apart, the earth and all that it contains will be burned up. (New Jerusalem Bible)

You might nod your head in recognition. You might say, "Well, those are the words of an uninformed layperson." But they do represent some reasonable assumptions we have made about a possible scenario for the planet earth.

With a cataclysmic astronomical event, with the predictable death of our local star, the sun, the sky will vanish as the oxygen and ozone are drawn off. The scientist might say that the fire and falling apart of the base elements is a primitive description of a nuclear explosion. But, most of all, scientists might express amazement with the realization that such a primitive, yet possible, prediction was made by a former fisherman who happened to live 2,000 years ago, and was a follower of Jesus — Simon Peter, by name.

Perhaps even more perplexing, in Peter's prediction, is the fact that the world was, by experience, a relatively stable platform on which to live. It shook occasionally with earthquakes, or erupted with volcanos and was inundated by floods, but generation after generation endured it, and had every reason to believe, by their experience, that it would always be that way.

Yet Ezekiel, Jesus, Peter, and John of Patmos, author of the book of Revelation, were convinced otherwise. They believed there was something else in the mind of God.

In order to comprehend that idea, which is in the mind of God, it would be helpful to orient ourselves as to where we are in this series of Lenten worship services on the "Sevenfold Path to Peace."

Last week, with the question, "Is peace attainable?" we suggested that the answer depends on our own willingness to recognize that wars start within ourselves and ripple out across the sea of humanity. Because Jesus had something else in mind, peace, he was able to project a quiet calm into nature itself, quieting the raging storm. Since that principle is true, we too, with peace in mind, could quiet the tempests which overwhelm our world. God has given us far more power to bring about what is in the Creator's mind than we have been willing to apply.

Today, in our search along the biblical Sevenfold Path to Peace, we find ourselves in a different place. If the peace which Jesus had in mind was able to calm the stormy sea of Galilee, then the peace which Peter sees in the mind of God is not ultimately the submission of nature, but its replacement with a new form, a nature not subject to decay, destruction, and turmoil. The new creation is inevitable . . . and it is peaceful. There is, in Peter, and you . . . and me, something which yearns for that time, beyond this earth's death.

But STOP!

The prophet Amos cries to us from the pages of the Old Testament a perplexing warning:

Woe to you who desire the day of the Lord! Why would you have the day of the Lord? It is darkness and not light. Amos 5:18

Amos waves the warning flag because he knows that what we live in the interim, between now and the day of the Lord, has an impact on us and on our world.

The little negativities we send out, like ripples from our minds, eventually strike some distant barrier and, with accumulating force, come back on us with terrible destructiveness.

Even that we which we imagine to be peace can have terrible consequences, because we want peace on our terms, not peace on God's terms.

What Amos lays bare in our minds is the fact that there is an inconsistency between what we profess, on the one hand, and do, on the other! Listen to his words,

> *Even though you offer me your burnt offerings and cereal offerings, I will not accept them, and the peace offerings of your fatted beasts I will not look upon. (Amos 5:22)*

Why would God not want our attempts at reconciliation and peace?

The answer is encapsulated in what God does want,

> *Let justice roll down like waters, and righteousness like an ever-flowing stream. (Amos 5:24)*

God is telling us, through Amos, that peace is something more than the desire to have a secure placid existence. Something more than a world without nature's destructive storms and humanity's manipulative control over the social order . . . a control which results in the denial of rights, which, in turn, leads to war.

Peace is the doing of justice.

In James Goldman's play, *The Lion In Winter,* from which I quoted last week, and in which Henry II is not only contending with the question of which of his three sons will succeed him on the throne, but also with the constant threat from France, he says;

Since Louis died, while Philip grew, I've had no France to fight. And in that lull, I've found how good it is to write a law or make a tax more fair, or sit in judgment to decide which peasant gets a cow. There is, I tell you, nothing more important in the world. And now the French boy's big enough and I'm sick of war.[1]

"To write a law or make a tax more fair, or to sit in judgment to decide which peasant gets a cow." "Let justice roll down like water and righteousness like an ever-flowing stream." That is the stuff peace is made of. That is what God has in mind . . . what God desires.

A person who has served on the field of battle in a war summarizes his experience like this: "War is brute force. On the battlefield there is no justice. Right does not prevail. There is no mercy. Land and people are destroyed. There is not any law, only chaos. Survival is largely a matter of chance. War is not fair. It is inhumane."

Perhaps it is easy for a congregation of people, even a nation of people, to brush off the words of preachers, spoken from the philosophical contemplations of their studies, or in pulpit reflections on biblical witness of ancient prophets. It is more compelling and persuasive to hear the plea for "peace-which-is-the-result-of-justice," from an individual who has survived the war! War does not create justice. Justice creates peace.

The Apostle Peter said, following his description of the end of the world, "But according to (God's) promise we wait for new heavens and a new earth in which righteousness dwells." (2 Peter 3:13) "In which righteousness dwells." That's the fairness of which Henry II spoke and for which he yearned.

If we hear Amos rightly, if we take Peter's vision of the new heavens and new earth seriously, then the conditions which cause us to be separated, estranged from God, the conditions which made war possible, are those conditions in which injustice is perpetuated.

It was true in Czarist Russia, Nazi Germany, and a myriad

of dictatorial regimes such as Batista's Cuba. It is logical to conclude that the injustices we foster will not only generate the storms of war; they will inevitably ripple out to the destruction of the earth itself, thus fulfilling Peter's pre-scientific description of the sky's disappearance and the breaking apart of the elements in fire.

No wonder Peter says to us,

Therefore, beloved, since you wait for these, be zealous to be found by him without spot or blemish, and at peace. (2 Peter 3:14)

God engages us in the work of justice, because, when all else is said and done, then the new order is established. The only thing which will remain, when the dust is settled, will be righteousness.

God wants, very much, for you and me to be participants in that new order, that new peace. It is possible only if we start our participation now. Desire peace with deeds of justice and we all might take the next step on the "Sevenfold Path to Peace."

---

1. *The Lion in Winter*, James Goldman, (Random House, N.Y. 1965, used by permission. Act 1 Scene 5.)

Scripture   **Lent 3**
    Psalm 34:1-3, 11-14
    Romans 14:13-23
    Jeremiah 8:8-15
    Matthew 5:9; 10:34-39

Peacemaking — Active, Not Passive

Prokofiev's Symphonic Tale for Children, *Peter and the Wolf,* tells of Peter's escapade into the meadow, mistakenly leaving the gate open behind him. While he carries on a chat with his friend, the bird, the duck, unnoticed, escapes through the open gate and goes for a swim in the pond. The little bird and duck get to arguing, "What kind of bird are you if you can't swim?" And all the while the cat is stealthily sneaking up on the bird on velvet paws. "Look out!" cries Peter. The bird escapes to the tree. Peter's grandfather retrieves the boy from the possible danger of a wolf coming out of the forest. Indeed, that is what happens. The duck, in its excitement, jumps out of the pond and is swallowed whole by the wolf. Peter, with rope in hand, climbs the wall around the yard, works his way into the tree where both cat and bird have taken refuge from the wolf. While the bird distracts the wolf by flying about his head, Peter makes a loop in the rope and snares the wolf, which is then marched off to the zoo, with the help of hunters, grandfather, cat, bird, and Peter leading the procession; and the duck, which was swallowed alive is quacking inside the wolf.

Written in 1936 in Moscow, one can only wonder if Prokofiev was making something more than a story for children. Perhaps it is a lightly veiled prophecy of international intrigue.

A six-year-old boy, listening to the story, snuggled up to his grandmother's side and, reflecting on Peter's carelessness at leaving the gate open, and his heroism in capturing the wolf, looking up said, "Grandma, can a person be bad and good at the same time?" The name for that possibility is "paradox." A paradox is a seemingly contradictory statement which may, nonetheless, be true.

In order to understand the role of paradox in the process of peace-making, it would be helpful to review the first two steps we have taken on "The Sevenfold Path to Peace," which we are pursuing during this period of Lent.

First, with the question, "Is peace Attainable?" we wrestled with the fact that what happens inside of us ultimately affects the world around us. The acquisition of world peace starts with our individual and collective inner peace with God.

Secondly, comes the desire for peace . . . not simply an unruffled calm sea of humanity acquiescing, or passively yielding, to the intimidations of a greater force, in the sense Poland has peace, but rather peace which is rooted and grounded in God's justice.

By these first two steps, I have sought to persuade you that peace is attainable and desirable.

It is also *intentional*.

That is the fundamental nature of the third step on the "Sevenfold Path to Peace." Peace is an activity — a purposeful activity. Peace does not just happen . . . it is made. But peace-making, by its very nature, can be divisive or disruptive of relationships. Therein lies the paradox.

Listen again as the words of Jesus are translated by Moffit;

Blessed are the peacemakers! They will be ranked with the (children) of God. (Matthew 5:9)

and yet, just five chapters later, Matthew recalls these paradoxical words of Jesus;

Never imagine I have come to bring peace on earth; I have not come to bring peace but a sword. I have come to set a man against his father, a daughter against her mother, a daughter-in-law against her mother-in-law; yes, a man's own household will be his enemies. He who loves father or mother more than me is not worthy of me; he who will not take his cross and follow me is not worthy of me. He who has found life will lose it, and he who loses his life for my sake will find it. (Matthew 10:34-39)

"Grandma, can you be bad and good at the same time? If the duck escapes through carelessness . . . the wolf is captured with careful planning.

In order for peace to be made, there must be careful planning, with a full acceptance of the fact that there is going to be a division of the house. There are those who will want to make peace on their terms and not on the terms suggested by Christ.

There is carved into the front-plate of the pulpit at a church in Hawaii, a sword pointed downward, overlaid with a dove carrying an olive branch flying upward. The Word of God, as it comes to us from the Bible, is like that. The sword slices away at every loyalty which hinders our relationship with Christ, and thereby, which inhibits the peace-making process.

The price of peace with justice came high and dear during the American Civil War, and yet Julia Ward Howe movingly captured the truth and cost of God's justice in the "Battle Hymn of the Republic."

*Mine eyes have seen the glory
Of the coming of the Lord;
He is trampling out the vintage
Where the grapes of wrath are stored.
He has loosed the fateful lightning
Of his terrible swift sword;
His truth is marching on.*

"I have not come to bring peace," said Jesus, "but a sword." The sword he brought was not that of war-making, but rather the division of justice from injustice. That is why the symbol of our national Justice Department has the blindfolded and impartial justice holding the balance scales in one hand and the sword in the other.

If we are to be peacemakers, then we must count the cost.

If we are to be peacemakers, we must also be intentionally personal about it. We cannot count on governments to initiate peace.

I would turn your minds again to James Goldman's play on which we have reflected during the past two weeks, *The Lion In Winter*. Aging Henry II of England is engaged in conversation with Philip of France, who, along with Henry's three sons, is in contention to succeed Henry on the throne of England.

> Henry says, "We are the world in small. A nation is a human thing; it does what we do, for our reasons. Surely, if we are civilized, it must be possible to put the knives away. We can make peace. We have it in our hands."[1]

There was a film on TV called "World War III." The main plot was the build-up of arms, the developing war between the U.S. and the Soviets, and the contentions between the hardliners and the moderates. The subplot was an individual battle between a Soviet company of soldiers and an American unit defending an oil pipeline pumping station in Alaska. The two commanding officers decided, in that remote outpost, that if peace was to start anywhere, it had to start with them. Just as they shook hands to make peace, one of the Soviet's lieutenants blew up the two officers. In the meantime, in Moscow and Washington, the hardliners were edging out the moderates and the buttons were pushed.

The scenes which followed were of everyday life in the Soviet Union and America. Parades and flags, barbecues and beaches — a stunning ending with persuasive impact — especially when you know that there are millions of tons of explosive power stored up in the nuclear arsenals of the Soviet Union and America (in fact more than several hundred pounds of explosive for each human being on the face of the earth).

And Jesus said, "Blessed are the peacemakers." Only

intentional peacemakers will stop such insanity. In doing so, we will count the cost of the sword which separates God's means of peacemaking from the military method.

If we are to be peacemakers, the Bible tells us that we must center on Christ. "He who loves (fatherland) or (motherland) more than me is not worthy . . ." We must center not on family, not on our own well-being, but on Christ. There can be peace in us and in our world, a peace which is uniquely different from the world's methodology, and political knee jerk philosophy.

A choir anthem, *Quiet Place*, describes God at the center. "There you will know . . . you will know." The Quakers call it "centering down."

Centering down is the proceess of working the inner soil, pulverizing it, and making it receptive for the seeds of peace, which the Holy Spirit would plant in us. Centering down is the process of recognizing the clumps and clods of fear and insecurity in ourselves, which distort the landscape of our souls.

It is paradoxical that such an inner and peaceful relationship can be established with God in the very midst of turmoil. Yet it is true. It is like a garden planted in the midst of the city, which provides a place of refuge and solace. In that quiet place, God nurtures the growth of inner peace which can then be carried out into the tumultuous world.

Let's sum up where we have come, thus far, in this series:
- It is possible to attain peace.
- The possibility begins to find its reality in the desire for justice.
- But the desire is not enough. Desire must be translated into action — peacemaking.
- The intention to make peace finds its reality when we first, count the cost; secondly, make it a personal effort and; thirdly, center ourselves in Christ.

Having come this far, we are now ready to take the next step on the Sevenfold Path to Peace.

Prayers of the Church

Quiet me down, O Lord, until all my inner strivings cease. Generate in me the powerful energies of peace. Take the anxious strivings, myriad doubts, and most hidden fears which drive the mechanisms of inner turmoil and world-wide wars; and, as in a chemical process, change their molecular structure until, at last, those same inner powers are dedicated to the peaceful purposes of your eternal realm.

Lord Jesus, who endured the constant assaults of the Evil One, by being ever alert to the opportunities to make peace, keep us, in like manner, vigilant, that no temptation to evil or injustice will overwhelm us.

We are frank to admit that we are tempted to wrap ourselves in a cocoon of isolation from the world and not think about our place in the peace-making process. With the advent of spring, make us a new creation, willing to test our wings, and ready to carry the good news of peace to all peoples.

We bring to our minds those people who do not have a just peace and who, therefore, are not at peace — people in Poland, Northern Ireland, the Middle East, Southeast Asia, Africa, Latin America.

And those who are afflicted in mind, body, or spirit, who are not at rest in you. In the words of the Psalmist, help us to

> *keep our tongue from evil and our lips*
> *from speaking deceit. Help us to depart*
> *from evil and do good. Help us to seek*
> *peace and pursue it.*

Make us happy, O Lord, in the work of peacemaking, even as you have promised, through Jesus Christ our Lord. Amen

---

1. *The Lion in Winter*, James Goldman, (Random House, N.Y. 1965, used by permission, Act 1, Scene 2).

Scripture:
Psalm 72:1-7
1 Peter 3:8-18
Isaiah 9:2-7
Luke 10:1-12

Lent 4

Peace as Shalom

Text: *"Peace be to this house." (Luke 10:5)*

Our bus pulled off the highway onto an overpass, where it stopped. The road up from Lod airport, near Tel Aviv, had displayed to us the remnants of the wars of Israel. Shelled-out tanks and armored personnel carriers were preserved where they had fallen, as memorials to the men who had fought and died there.

Now our eyes were turned eastward, where we could see our first view of Jerusalem. The tour guide invited me to offer prayer. It is only from the vantage point of a year later, that I can now place a little round-headed pin on the map of my life-journey, to mark that spot as a particularly significant point in life.

There, with a group of Phoenix civic and religious leaders, I was granted the rare privilege and emotionally moving opportunity to lead Christians and Jews in prayer to a common God. The words of Psalm 122 came to mind,

Pray for the peace of Jerusalem:
May they prosper who love you!
Peace be within your walls, and
security within your towers!
For my brethren and companions' sake
I will say, "Peace be within you!"

There is more in the name Jerusalem than meets the eye of those of us who speak only English. In popular Jewish thought (if not in the technical analysis of root words), Jerusalem comes from two words: "Jeru" — which means "foundation or city," and "Shalem" — which means "whole or complete."

Foundation of wholeness . . . city of completeness. But even more important, for our consideration today, is the fact that from the word Shalem or Salem, comes the word "Shalom" — Peace.

> *Pray for the Shalom of the city of wholeness.*
> *Shalom be within your walls.*
> *Shalom be to this house.*
> *City of Peace!*

In order to orient you as to where we are on the "Sevenfold Path to Peace" which we have been taking on this Lenten series of worship services, let's briefly take a look back.

First, with the question, "Is peace attainable?" we determined that the answer lies within each one of us, for it is first in our minds that war and peace are made.

Secondly, the path leads us to the desirability of peace, specifically as it grows out of our own need for justice, and the need of the world for justice. Where there is no justice, there is no peace.

Thirdly, we arrived at the place of peace-making, recognizing that there is a price to be paid, an intentional personal effort to be made and, most fundamentally, Christ to be centered on.

Today's step is that of Shalom.

Frederick Buechner, Vermont's resident interpreter of biblical concepts, writes of peace in his book, *Wishful Thinking*,

> *Peace has come to mean that time when there aren't any wars or even when there aren't any major wars. Beggars can't be choosers; most of us settle for that. But in Hebrew peace,* **Shalom,** *means fullness, means having everything you need to be wholly and happily yourself . . . for Jesus peace seems to have meant not the absence of struggle but the presence of love.*[1]

Harold Wilke is a man who was born without arms. It was not possible to fit him with artificial limbs. He told me of an incident when he was about six years old. A neighbor lady was visiting his mother. Harold was continuing the process of learning to use his feet to care for himself, including feeding himself, which he does with graceful dexterity. But, on that particular occasion, he was attempting to put on a shirt and having an awful time of it. His mother, with pursed lips and clenched hands, was using every ounce of will power to resist helping him in his protracted struggle. The neighbor, not fully comprehending, said to Harold's mother, "Don't you love him enough to help?" To which his mother replied, with tears in her eyes, "I am helping him."

Shalom is love which teaches self-reliance. That kind of love is fundamental to personal peace and worldly peace.

Secondly, Shalom is peace with self-discipline.

A man came recently, seeking counsel. An acquaintance from some years prior was in jail, and had appealed to my friend to put up some collateral for bail-bond. The detained man, in his twenties, had a history of minor felonies.

"He just has never grown up," said my friend.

"Why not?" I inquired.

"Well, his father belongs to the Mafia. And he has always made it easy for him . . . but I think if I showed him some Christian love, I could help turn him around. That's what the Bible seems to be telling me."

My friend had been through an agonizing personal struggle with drugs and lack of self-discipline. At one point, other people had had to govern his life because he refused to rule his own behavior.

"What changed you?" I asked.

"When God taught me that I was going to lose everything if I kept running away."

"What does your friend in jail need most?"

"To confront the reality of his behavior," said my visitor.

"Will bail-bond help?"

He smiled, embraced me, and said, "I know now what not to do."

God's Shalom, with which we are entrusted, helps to stabilize those who will learn from the firmness of love which cares enough to set limits.

Thirdly, Shalom is a *gift* of peace from God.

These are the instructions Jesus gave to the seventy disciples he sent out to do the work of faith.

> *Carry no purse, no bag, no sandals; and salute no one on the road, Whatever house you enter, first say, "Peace be to this house!" And if a (child) of peace is there, your peace shall rest upon (that person); but if not, it shall return to you.*

Jesus went on to describe the horrible consequences of rejecting the peace which is brought by God's servants.

Shalom is not a casual greeting, not simply a word of farewell, like "Hello!" or "Goodbye!" The salute, the verbal greeting, and salutation are ways of displaying the fact that the greeter is unarmed and intends no evil. With them, we say, "Don't worry, friend, I'm not going to attack."

Shalom is more profound than that. When I offer you Shalom, I am giving you God's love that is in me. Shalom is intensely personal and caring. It is not casual, but carries with it the power of healing. The people who are vehicles of Shalom convey the essence of God's Holy Spirit to others. It is self-giving.

Those who refuse the gift condemn themselves, according to Jesus. It is not that God will pour out Divine vengeance on them, but that they have refused to accept God's Shalom. By definition, the absence of God is the absence of peace. That is a real definition of hell!

Although I've described Shalom in terms of love which teaches self-reliance, self-discipline, and self-giving, the focus on self is not really accurate. The focus is really on God. Reliance on God, discipline by God, and giving to God.

Shalom is, then, fulfillment in God.

A woman who worshiped with us, for some months, in the knowledge of her approaching death, provided me with a copy of the composition which was found in St. Paul's Church in Baltimore in 1692. Its unknown author captures something of the essence of God's fulfilling Shalom.

"Go placidly amid the noise and haste and remember what peace there may be in silence as far as possible without surrender. Be on good terms with all persons. Speak your truth quietly and clearly and listen to others, even the dull and ignorant, for they too have their story.

"Avoid loud and aggressive persons, they are vexations to the spirit. If you compare yourself with others, you may become vain and bitter, for always there will be greater and lesser persons than yourself.

"Enjoy your achievements as well as your plans. Keep interested in your career, however humble; it is a real possession in the changing fortune of time. Exercise caution in your business affairs; for the world is full of trickery, but let this not blind you to what virtue there is; many persons strive for high ideals and everywhere life is full of heroism.

"Be yourself, expecially do not feign affection. Neither be cynical about love; for in the face of acridity and dis-enchantment it is as perennial as the grass. Take kindly the counsel of years, gracefully surrendering the things of youth.

"Nurture strength of spirit to shield you from sudden misfortune, but do not distress yourself with imaginings; many fears are borne out of distress and loneliness.

"Beyond a wholesome discipline, be gentle with yourself, you are a child of God of the Universe . . . No less than a tree or the stars, you have a right to be here and whether or not it is clear to you, no doubt the universe is unfolding as it should, therefore be at peace with God whatever you conceive him to be and whatever your labor or aspirations.

"In the noisy confusion of life, keep peace with your soul with all its shames, and broken dreams. It is still a beautiful world . . ."

- *Shalom is the peace of Godly fulfillment.*
- *Shalom is love which teaches Godly reliance.*
- *Shalom is peace which comes with Godly discipline.*
- *Shalom is peace which comes with Godly giving.*
- *Shalom is attainable and desirable.*
- *Shalom is intentional and loving.*

Now we are ready to take the next step on the *Sevenfold Path to Peace*.

Prayers of the Church

Lord, teach me to love.
Teach me to love in such a way and with so much caring, that those I love can stand on their own, creating no burden for others . . . but Lord, when by reason of circumstance, they can no longer stand, still let me love — love with Shalom, so I will have the strength of your love to bear the load.
Lord, teach me self-discipline.
Teach me self-discipline in the little things that I might be strong in the big things. Stay me from temptation, especially the temptation of leaping to the rescue of those who need to work out their own solutions. But Lord, when, by reason of circumstance, I see wrong being done, still let me love, love with Shalom which does not yield to the temptation to stand aloof and allow evil to go on unhindered.
Lord, teach me to give.
Teach me to give so much of the essence of yourself, that my giving will heal the recipient, bring wholeness and completeness to my environment, and will generate peace on earth. But Lord, when, by reason of circumstance, the gift is rejected, stay me from the temptation of vindictiveness, hate, or hostility, that

I might live in the confidence of Shalom which knows that all things under the heavens are subject to your governance.

Lord, teach me of fulfillment.

Teach me of the fulfillment of Shalom, that with peace in my heart, mind, and relationships, I might lend fulfillment to others. But Lord, when I encounter those who are empty, stay me from the temptation of judging them unworthy of Shalom, so I might bring Shalom to them, in the manner of Jesus. Shalom, Shalom. Amen

---

1. *Wishful Thinking,* by Frederick Buechner (used by permission, Harper and Row, N.Y., 1973, p. 69.)

Scripture: **Lent 5**
   Psalm 37:1-4; 37-40
   Ephesians 2:11-22
   2 Chronicles 14:1-7
   John 14 (selections)

The Gift of Peace

Text: *"Peace I leave with you; my peace I give to you; not as the world gives do I give to you."*
John 14:27

At the drive-in window of the bank there is a pneumatic tube. The transaction slips, checks, and money are put in a capsule, which is dropped into the tube. As air is sucked out from in front of the capsule and pressured behind it, the container is pushed through the tube. I used the tube one day.

It came as no surprise to me, then that a pneumatic tube showed up in a dream, in which I was attempting to assemble a clear plastic tube. The problem in the dream was that, at one point, the tube divided into two parts like separating railroad tracks, which then had to be brought back together again further along, but didn't fit properly. Worse than that, I was conscious in the dream that I was being pressured through the tube and was going to have to go through the divided portion, while still being one person.

Not much interpretation was required. The previous day I had visited a grieving family in the morning, conducted a wedding service, and attended the reception in the afternoon, and then gone back to write a funeral service, while thinking about getting out of town for thirty-two hours of rest.

Life is sometimes like a pneumatic tube which pressures us along, divides our commitments and emotions, and forces us to find a way to make all the pieces fit, without being totally divided.

If the lives of others sometimes feel like mine in the dream, is it any wonder that personal peace and world peace are so hard to come by?

The Sevenfold Path to Peace which we have been pursuing during Lent is not a pneumatic tube pressuring us along, but there are compelling forces which clearly indicate that, if we fail to find the path to peace, our encapsulated spaceship earth is going to be propelled into the vacuum of oblivion by the sheer pressure of world armaments.

Richard Barnet, Director of the Institute for Policy Studies in Washington, D.C., reports that in 1980 almost $1.5 billion a day was spent on armaments by the nations of the world, for a total of over $560 billion a year, in the name of peace!

Our Lenten path has sought to lead us, not in the high pressure of peace through armaments, but through the carefully measured steps of a personal inner search, an evaluation of our world environment, and the biblical imperatives for peace.

We have determined that peace is attainable, that because of the human need for justice, it is desirable, that peacemaking must be intentional, and that it is based on God's Shalom, love, which is reliable, disciplined, giving, and fulfilling.

Today we focus on the fifth step to peace: What must we do to get out of the pneumatic tube?

How are we able to receive the gift of peace?

Jesus said,

Peace I leave with you, my peace I give to you; not as the world gives do I give to you. Let not your hearts be troubled, neither let them be afraid. (John 14:27)

If I don't have peace, the peace which Jesus gives, and if the world does not have Jesus' peace, then it must be due to the fact that we are doing something wrong. Our receptors are bad, like radio receivers tuned only to static.

The biblical material we have heard today gives us three clues as to how to get back on the path of peace, to receive what God is offering so we need not live in the pneumatic tube.

First, consider some of the words of Psalm 37 with which our service opened:

Vs. 1 "Fret not yourself because of the wicked, be not envious of wrongdoers."
Vs. 3 "Trust in the Lord, and do good so you will dwell in the land and enjoy security."
Vs. 37 "Mark the blameless man, and behold the upright, there is posterity for the man of peace."

If we are going to receive Christ's peace, then we are necessarily going to have to stop worrying, start trusting, start doing good, and make note of the people who make peace, because it is their descendants who will survive, and not the descendants of war makers.

That's all well and good, but the fact is that I do worry, I have a hard time trusting God; "do-gooders" don't enjoy any popularity and peace-makers can't ever win a political office which carries any clout. It is nearly impossible to live in the world on the terms of peace suggested by the Psalmist.

In Pennsylvania there is a retreat center known as Kirkridge, which for years has been a vital place of helping people become more contemplative and spiritually centered.

Robert Raines, a former Methodist bishop and director of the center said, in an interview about the role of Kirkridge in peace-making,

Obviously hostile people can't make a peaceful world. So we have got to work both the inward and outward dimensions. So, while some of our current emphasis is directed toward seeking a mutual nuclear arms freeze, nuclear disarmament, because that appears to be a growing urgency, we are also concerned for being a place on this mountainside where people can acknowledge their angers, their fears, their grief, and so become peaceable people.[1]

I hear Raines suggesting that the fundamental clue to receiving the peace which Jesus gives in a manner different from the world, is acknowledgment. Confession . . . of our anger, our fear, our grief. It is these things which drive the pneumatic tube propelling us toward the loss of all future generations.

"God help me, I'm angry, fearful, grieving . . ." This honest assessment of our innermost motivators is fundamental to clearing away the impediments to finding the *Sevenfold Path to Peace*. Until I admit there is something wrong in me, I do not allow God to make something right in me.

The second biblical clue is found in the 2 Chronicles 14 story of Asa, whose land was free from war and at peace for ten years. Listen:

> *He did what was good and right in the eyes of the Lord his God. He took away the foreign altars and the high places and broke down pillars and hewed down the Asherim, and commanded Judah to seek the Lord, the God of their Fathers, and to keep the law and the commandment.*

Asa tore down the objects of worship which diverted attention from God, and he did what was right and good. Consequently he was able to say,

> *the land is still ours, because we have sought the Lord our God; we have sought him, and he has given us peace on every side.*

The god of modern society is like the Asherim, the cultic god; it is not the supreme God of all creation, not the God revealed in Jesus of Nazareth and the Holy Spirit. Our modern god is named "Security."

"Security" is the object of our worship, the worship of the nations — the foreign altars are aircraft carriers, the high places are spy satellites, the pillars are intercontinental ballistic missiles, the cultic gods, the modern Asherim are firearms which are coveted by a fearful society.

Any mere hint of suggestion that the nations start reversing the arms race results in clear evidence of where their commitment lies and what god is worshiped. That is the way the world gives peace, or what the world calls peace.

"Peace I leave with you, my peace I give to you, not as the world gives do I give to you," said Jesus. If we Christians are to be agents of that peace, then we must convince the Asas of the world, the leaders of the world, to tear down the accouterments, the trappings, the symbols of worship of a false god, the god "Security," as appealing as that god may seem to be.

Thirdly, we have heard in Ephesians these words:

For (Jesus) is our peace, who has made us both one, and has broken down the divinding wall of hostility . . . He came and preached peace to you who were far off and peace to those who were near; for through him we both have access in one Spirit to the Father. So then you are no longer strangers and sojourners, but you are fellow citizens with the saints and members of the household of God . . . (Ephesians 2:14-19)

If we are going to be recipients of the gift of peace, then our world view must change.

A man asked me whether or not our church was going to provide refuge for El Salvadorians, as churches in Tucson are doing in defiance of the Immigration and Naturalization Service. During the ensuing discussion, I told him that fundamental to the position of the Tucson group, is the concept of world community.

In Christendom there are no political boundaries, no racial barriers, no foreign language, no opposing economies. Christianity sees a world community, and lives as if world community is the reality. Christianity believes that God's realm is the only and ultimate reality. From God's point of view the dividing walls of hostility are broken down through Jesus Christ.

That is the peace which Jesus gives. It is not a kind of peace the world gives, but we could receive it if we confess our anger, fear, and grief.

We could receive it if we stopped worshiping the false god named "Security."

We could receive the gift of peace if we began to see the world as God sees it,

> *the whole structure is joined together and grows into a holy temple in the Lord; in whom you also are built into it for a dwelling place of God in the Spirit.*

Receive the gift of peace, and together we will be ready to take the next step on the *Sevenfold Path to Peace.*

Prayer

Lord Jesus, we are so eager to receive your peace, peace which is far different from our worldly understanding of peace . . . peace which is made, not defensively, but creatively, lovingly, intentionally, and justly.

I admit that there is anger in me which is something more than righteous indignation, an anger which inflicts its hurt on others. And there is fear which aggressively attacks, lest the source of that fear gets the upper hand. And there is grief which blames and accuses because it knows not how to bear the pain to seek solace.

Forgive me, Lord, for the misguided results of my anger, fear, and grief.

Almighty God, by whose authority and permission alone, the rulers of the earth maintain their offices of responsibility, we implore you to inspire them to tear down the worldly temples of worship to the false god, Security, and all the decorations of those temples, replacing them with the symbols of creativity, love, and justice.

Spirit of the living God, who dwells both beyond and in our

very being, help us now to rise above our world and see it as you see, one world community governed by your authority alone . . . and, in the seeing, help us to realize that you are our forgiveness, our security, and our everlasting source of peace, through Jesus Christ. Amen

1. From *Catalyst Tape Talk*, by Robert Raines (Vol. 13, Number 6, 1980, used by permission of Word Books, Publisher, Waco, TX 76796.)

Scripture:
 Psalm 85:8-13
 Zechariah 9:9-12
 Luke 19:29-44

Lent 6
Palm Sunday

Peace Through Sacrifice

Text: *"Would that even today you knew the things that make for peace."*

I have held in my hand the only known existing acheological evidence in the world, that crucifixion was actually practiced, as the Bible and other literature asserts.

At the Rockefeller Museum in Jerusalem, Joe Zias, a nephew to one of our group and custodian of the Dead Sea Scrolls, handed to us a hand-wrought iron spike about six inches long and with the tip bent over at right angles. There were some fragments of wood on the spike, but most startling was the fact that the spoke had been driven directly through an ankle bone.

Apparently, when the victim was crucified, the spike had struck a hard knot in the upright beam and had bent over. When his family went to retrieve the body for burial, they could not pull out the spike and had to cut off the beam and bury a portion of it with the spike still in place through the ankle.

It is doubtful that any of us could be any more in touch with the sheer brutality and pain and suffering of crucifixion than I was when I held that spike in my hand and looked at the ancient bone. The self-offering of God, in that moment, took on for me, a more harsh reality.

The Lord of the universe is willing and has always been willing to take on the most brutal aspects of humanity in order to hold a mirror up to our face. In the reflection, God intends that we will not be pleased with what we see, and will then make the decisions to choose a better way.

It is that better way, which is the *Sevenfold Path to Peace* we have been pursuing during these Sundays in Lent. Thus far, it has been my purpose to convince you of the following:

- Peace is attainable because it starts within us.
- Peace is desirable because we all need justice.
- Peacemaking does not just happen, it is intentional.
- Peace is Shalom, God's tough love.
- Peace is receivable when we confess our anger, fear, and grief, when we stop worshiping the false god named Security, and when we gain a world view, such as God has, which sees beyond our short-sighted human barriers.

Today's step on the Sevenfold Path is the sixth, which suggests that peace comes through sacrifice.

First, some biblical perspective.

Jesus approached Jerusalem on Palm Sunday from the east. He arrived from Bethany, having come around the southern flank of the Mount of Olives, through the olive grove, such as the one still there on the edge of the Kidron Valley. According to Luke's rendition of the story, it would have been in that vicinity he would have received the enthusiastic greetings from the crowd shouting,

Blessed is the King who comes in the name of the Lord! Peace in heaven and glory in the highest.

But remember, there is no evidence that Jesus gave anything, but the most sober response, to hopes he raised among the people. He continued up the road which runs from south to north from the valley, traversing the hill to the Golden Gate. Ancient tradition holds that it is through the gate which the King of Israel entered to assume his authority. Some centuries ago, the Moslems bricked up the gate, so no one could go through it and claim kingship over them. Even while I was there I saw a Moslem guard chase a tourist away from it.

Jesus entered through the Golden Gate, and was carried up the ramp on the inside by his young animal, to the level of the Temple courtyard.

Most certainly he had in mind the words of Zechariah the

prophet, who set the stage with the picture of such a humble entry, and then said of Jerusalem:

> *I will cut off the chariot from Ephraim and the war horse from Jerusalem; and the battle bow shall be cut off, and he shall command peace to the nations; his dominion shall be from sea to sea, and from the River to the ends of the earth.*

No wonder Jesus, then able to see the rest of the city to the south and west, wept and said,

> *Would that even today you knew the things that make for peace! But now they are hid from your eyes . . .*

Jesus knew, as did Zechariah before him, that peace is not made from either ancient or modern chariots, war horses, or battle bows.

What was hid from their eyes was that the peace which Jesus would command from the River Jordan to the ends of the earth, would be the result of his approaching sacrifice. What is especially germane to this series of sermons, and which we often miss in the celebration of Palm Sunday, is that peace was at the very center of the prophecy of the event, and foremost in the mind of Jesus.

"Would that even today you knew the things that make for peace."

Jesus already had in mind the final sacrifice which had to be made in order that his authority would extend to the ends of the earth. He had to have known that part of that sacrifice was a hand-wrought iron spike through the ankle bone.

Secondly, it will be helpful to understand something of the nature of sacrifice . . .

Frederick Buechner, my favorite theological wordsmith, makes it short and simple:

SACRIFICE — to sacrifice something is to make it holy by giving it away for love.[1]

We've grown up with the idea that a sacrifice is hard to do, even painful, that it is done with great reluctance, if not actually extracted from us by intimidation or outright threat.

Sacrifice in Buechner's terms, and, indeed, in biblical terms, sees beyond the short term loss, beyond the security of possession, beyond the sentimentality of retention. Sacrifice is more nearly the willing offering of all one has, all one is . . . for the sake of the long-range vision, because the vision is so much more hopeful, fulfilling, satisfying, than the short term suffering.

Jesus was not above suffering or pain. He wept for the city, not only because of what it would suffer for having failed to recognize him, but for himself, because he knew what they would put him through. Later in the week, he agonized in the garden of Gethsemane over his approaching sacrifice. And, believe me, he suffered when that wrought-iron spike was driven through his ankle bone.

But Jesus also knew that he had to give life away for the love of you and me. It was in the giving that he made life holy for all of us.

Thirdly, the problem for you and me is one of how we go about appropriating Christ's sacrifice, which, in theological circles, is called the Atonement. That means, "at one ment."

Jesus said, "Would that even today you knew the things that make for peace! But now they are hid from your eyes."

What are those things which are hid from our eyes? The fact is — peace already exists! The problem is that we have not come to grips with that fact!

We have not opened our eyes to the reality of peace.

We have been unaware of the time of our visitation.

We have been tempted to believe that peace will be the result of our personal persuasion, our political power, our military maneuvering, or the individual and collective sacrifices we make to that end.

The fundamental conviction of Christians through the centuries has been that, through the sacrifice of Jesus, the chasm between ourselves and God has been bridged, and, in faith, we have been reunited with God. Therefore, what we do does not create peace, but affirms the peace which already is!

There is no fear of failure, no overwhelming anxiety, no angry or prideful reaction to a world which will not accept peace on our terms. Rather, there is a quiet certainty, a willing offering of one's being, because peace is at the Center.

Jesus is our Peace. His sacrifice has taken away the pain of our offering, so there can be peace in us. Our sacrifice is then, one bringing Christ to others . . . by finding peace in ourselves, by being just, by being intentional, with Shalom, and with receptivity to peace on God's terms.

We symbolize that kind of peace month after month in our sacrament of Holy Communion. After the Prayer of Consecration of the elements, the congregation offers itself to God . . .

In the strength Christ gives we offer ourselves to you, giving thanks that you have called us to serve you.

That is our sacrifice. It is the giving ourselves over to him who is peace, that peace might be within us, and thereby in the world.

When you and I have made this offering of ourselves to God, that Christ might be in us, we will then be ready to take the final step on the *Sevenfold Path to Peace.*

---

1. *Wishful Thinking*, Frederick Buechner (Harper & Row, 1973, New York, p. 83, used by permission).

Scripture:
   Isaiah 57:14-19
   John 20:19-23
   Colossians 1:1-2, 15-20

Easter Sunday

Proclaim Peace

Text: *"Peace be with you."*

The run-of-the-mill soldier belonged to a surly lot in the Tenth Roman Legion which occupied Israel in the days of Jesus. The soldier probably had been pressed into duty involuntarily. His assignment to this back-water outpost of the empire was nearly an insult. With the exception of the occasional threat of a riot, the duty was terribly boring.

Amusement was hard to come by. Life had little value; so this scurrilous lot took some perverted joy in appropriating, for their entertainment, an ancient Persian game called "basilica." The evidence of the game is still visible in Jerusalem. About twelve to fifteen feet below the present level of the Via Dolorosa, and in the subbasement of one of the Christian shrines commemorating the Stations of the Cross, archeologists have laid bare paving stones, roughly four feet square, which may be the actual street on which Jesus walked.

On some of those stones along the roadway are chiseled game boards with the markings of a basilica. The name referred not to a form of church building known as the basilica, but rather to its root word from the Greek which means "king." The idea of the game was that, at the end of a full week of playing with dice-like devices, the loser would be declared King for a day — the day always happened to be Friday. They would dress the loser like a king, tease him, and then crucify him!

The game continued after the crucifixion to see who would get his possessions. One week, nearly two thousand years ago, the loser happened to get very lucky, because coincidently, another gruesome drama was being played out between Jewish authorities and the Roman governor. The question of who was *basileus* (king) swirled around one Jesus of Nazareth. When the game was over and it seemed expeditious to Pontius Pilate to quell the unrest of the Jerusalemites, by crucifying Jesus, the loser of the army's game suddenly found that there was a substitute victim who was treated as every loser had been treated week after week, with mock kingship, royal robe, crown, and scoffing salutations, and, with his crucifixion, gambling for his clothes.

Of course, that motley and contemptible lot, which esteemed life so lowly, could not have begun to comprehend that they were playing a game of much higher stakes, wagering on the fate of the Roman Empire and participating, unwittingly, in the salvation, not only of the lottery loser, but of all humanity.

Remember playing King of the Mountain on piles of snow or heaps of sand, when you were a kid? In many ways the nations of the world continue to play a modern version of king for the week. One week the game is played on the Falkland Islands, another in Israel, continuously in Lebanon, El Salvador, Ireland, or in southeast Asia.

During the Sundays of Lent we have been reflecting on the means by which we can stop playing those silly games of basilica, with their inevitable violent life-wasting endings. We have called the series *The Sevenfold Path to Peace*.

1. The first step was to acknowledge that, just as wars feed on the wars within us, so does peace find its beginning within us.

2. The second step was one of seeing that justice is fundamental to the desirability of peace. Peace without justice is no peace at all.

3. The third step, that of peace-making, demands that we plan for peace. It does not just happen anymore than war "just" happens . . . peace is intentional.

4. The fourth step of peace is God's Shalom, God's reliant, disciplining, giving, fulfilling love.

5. The fifth step, that of receiving Shalom's peace, requires that we confess our fear, anger, grief; that we stop worshiping the false god named "Security," and that we see the world and its peoples as a unitary whole, as God sees us.

6. The sixth step was the realization that peace already exists. It has been established through the sacrifice of Jesus. To accept Christ, is to have peace.

That brings us to the seventh step.

How can we get other people and the rest of the world to know the fact of peace so there will be peace?

The answer is at the heart of the resurrection experience. Your experience of the resurrection of Jesus establishes peace in terms we have been describing. The first encounter of the disciples with the resurrected Lord *pointed them toward proclaiming peace to the world.* It is the Easter imperative . . . the Easter urgency . . . the Easter realization that the kingdom of God is established. That is such remarkably good news anyone who has realized it cannot help but share it. It is in the sharing that peace will come.

Jesus' words to the disciples, that evening, essentially were in four commands.

First he said: "Peace be with you."
He did not say, "The fear of your enemies be with you."
He did not say, "The doubt about the economy be with you."
He did not say, "The stockpile of weapons be with you."
He did not say, "The bounty of the wealthy be with you."
He did not say, "The law be with you."
He said, "Peace be with you."

In light of what we concluded last week, that is the same

as saying, "Christ be with you, . . . in you . . . through you."

Perhaps you, like I, are tempted to look at the worst possible scenario with regard to earth's future: environmental decay, possibility of war, or something more personal like the plight of a sick relative.

Easter says, stop giving energy to the negatives. Use the energies of Christ for the positively creative. The resurrection encounter of the disciples was no theological doctrine, no philosophical teaching, subject to doubt and debate; it was the vivid experience of realizing that God is the victor in the perverse game of basilica. Easter calls us to start living on God's terms, positively.

"Peace be with you."

The second command of the resurrection experience is this:

As the Father has sent me, even so I send you.

With peace in them, the followers of Jesus are sent out to be Peace. It does not take a terribly perceptive person to know that the world is largely ignorant of the means of making peace. The Church has borne a major responsiblity for that ignorance. The Academy Award-winning film, *Chariots of Fire,* helped to clarify that fact for me. The Church, as it was institutionalized in the academic system of England at Cambridge, looked with contempt on the abilities of the young runner Jacobson, because he was a Jew. Even the homecoming from his 1924 Olympic victory in Paris left him out of the victory parade.

As long as the Church has operated with the official sanction of governments and institutions, and, at times, has actually controlled the body politic, it has become confused in its own mind and in the mind of the public, with the prevailing sociological, economic, and political attitudes of the culture, while aligning itself on one side or the other in the clashes of worldly forces.

Thank God, we are increasingly disentangling ourselves from that morass of modern crusade making. We are increasingly free to fulfill the mission on which Christ has sent us, that of proclaiming peace, doing justice, healing the people of the earth.

As the Father has sent me, even so I send you.

The third imperative of the Easter commission is found in these words of Jesus:

Receive the Holy Spirit.

To do that is to let the power of God be in you, transform you, work through you.
- There are some things you and I do because, "If I don't, who will?" — take out the garbage, do the dishes . . .
- There are some things you and I do because we "should" — vote on election day, stop at red lights . . .
- There are some things you and I do because it is expected of us: make your bed, make coffee for the after-church fellowship hour . . .
- There are some things you and I do because we want to: go four-wheeling, go to work . . .

But when we receive the Holy Spirit, there are some things you and I do, not because of obligations, expectations, or even personal wants. To have the Holy Spirit is to do God's thing because you can't help doing it. It is rather like falling in love . . . feeling all the excitement, and stimulation, and energy, and joy which makes life really alive, and unbounded by the limitations which usually seem to apply.

To receive the Holy Spirit is to be filled with the creative power of peace which nothing can sidetrack.

Receive the Holy Spirit.

The fourth aspect of the commission to Proclaim Peace, is that of forgiveness.

I was really struck by the King James Version of Jesus' words:

> *Whose soever sins ye remit, they are remitted unto them; and whose soever sins ye retain, they are retained.*

I've tended to think of forgiveness in terms of the effect it has on the person who committed the offense. But the word "remit," or give back, or cancel out, as it is used here, suddenly made me aware that the problem is really not for the doer of evil, but for the one to whom it is done!

If you hurt me and I keep that hurt, then there is trouble in it for me. I, then, carry a grudge. I, then, cannot possibly see you as a person worthy of love. I will not make peace with you . . . cannot make peace with you, because I have let your un-peace occupy my being.

Peace must start with the offended, the aggrieved, offering forgiveness.

So it is that the apparent loser in the cosmic game of basilica, first offered peace . . . peace be with you, to save the world.

This, then, is where the Sevenfold Path to Peace has brought us, not to the end of a path, but to a beginning. The Spirit in me prays that you will join me on the highway of our God . . .

> *"Bank up a causeway, clear a path, remove the stones from my people's way," says the Lord.*
>
> (Moffit translation)

" 'Peace, peace to the far and to the near,' says the Lord; 'and I will heal them.' "

Prayers of the Church

Almighty Lord Jesus, live now in us, in the confidence of faith; help us to embrace the reality of your Peace, as it is already established. Indeed, let the Peace of God which passes all understanding, the resurrection life, find a home in us . . . in the person next to me . . . in me.

Now help us to hear your clarion call to service, sending us, as you sent your disciples to the world, that the whole world might know, without prejudice of your Shalom, your peace, through us.

Grant each person sitting in this room, your Holy Spirit, that as your healing love transforms us to eminently hopeful people, undeterred by the problems of the world, we might faithfully fulfill your intentions.

Then stay us from retaining the sins of any, that we might see beyond our prejudices and assumptions, and instead, love each person according to need, until at last there is Peace on earth, as in heaven. Amen

www.ingramcontent.com/pod-product-compliance
Lightning Source LLC
Chambersburg PA
CBHW071800040426
42446CB00012B/2649